COLOR, COMMUNISM AND COMMON SENSE

by

MANNING
JOHNSON

FOREWORD BY ARCHIBALD B. ROOSEVELT

Contents

Copyright
ALLIANCE, INC.
New York, 1958

First Printing
May, 1958

Printed by
THE STUYVESANT PRESS CORP.
New York

MANNING JOHNSON

[1]

Soviet Agents Plot to Use U.S. Courts to Aid Communism

(1) Excerpts from the red pamphlet "UNDER ARREST."

Once and for all, it is necessary to destroy the illusions that workers have concerning courts and court procedure generally.

The "dignity" and "sanctity" of the courts are a means of paralyzing the struggle of the workers against capitalist institutions.

The Class Struggle Goes on in the Court Room

The class struggle goes on in the court room as well as it does on the picket line, in the shops, and in the mines.

Make the Court Your Forum

Bring out the class issues at the trial. In most cases

A most important consideration of workers' self-defense as already mentioned, is to use the capitalist courtroom as a forum from which the workers on trial*

1. These quotes are from a communist pamphlet published upon the orders from Moscow, in 1931, issued by Helena Stassova, an official of the Communist International. (Reference *Labor Defender*, a communist magazine, Oct. 1931, page 191.)

(2) Ex-President Theodore Roosevelt's letter to Felix Frankfurter, now a Supreme Court Justice, in 1917, criticises Frankfurter for supporting "traitors," "Bolsheviks" and "murderers."

Oyster Bay, December 19, 1917

My dear Mr. Frankfurter: I thank you for your frank letter.¹ I answer it at length because you have taken, and are taking, on behalf of the Administration an attitude which seems to me to be fundamentally that of Trotsky and the other Bolsheviki leaders in Russia; an attitude which may be fraught with mischief to this country.

Here again you are engaged in excusing men precisely like the Bolsheviki in Russia, who are murderers and encouragers of murder, who are traitors to their allies, to democracy, and to civilization, as well as to the United States, and whose acts are nevertheless apologized for on grounds, my dear Mr. Frankfurter, substantially like those which you allege.**

2. Theodore Roosevelt (26th President of the United States) uttered a prophetic warning about Felix Frankfurter, who today is the main influence behind the Supreme Court majority.

*Pamphlet *Under Arrest*, a standard communist textbook for many years.

**Letter from Theodore Roosevelt to Felix Frankfurter, December 19, 1917.

PREFACE

In modern literature, anti-communists are generally pictured as scoundrels. On the other hand, left-wing Perjurers and Jail Birds are shown as persecuted lambs.* But there is a special vitriol uncorked for those who have followed communism, and have repented to such an extent that they are publicly willing to stand up and testify against it by word and deed.

The writer of this pamphlet, Manning Johnson, is an example of such treatment. The Supreme Court of the United States used a communist statement in a decision of the majority opinion, as delivered by Justice Felix Frankfurter** to brand Manning Johnson as giving "tainted" testimony and cited as a basis for this statement the Communist Party brief.*** The left-wing papers, including the *New York Herald Tribune* joyfully took up the cry. Of course, careful investigation shows that Manning Johnson is not a perjurer, and it would be easy to prove this in any court not dominated by such a character as Felix Frankfurter.****

Manning Johnson's story begins very much like many other Negroes brought up in a religious home. He was inducted into the "party" largely because of the preachings of a communist Bishop (retired) of the Episcopal church, William Montgomery Brown. Manning Johnson is a man

---

* As examples, see the *New York Times, New York Herald Tribune,* and *Saturday Review of Literature* treatments of Hiss and Oppenheimer.
** See "Decision April 30th, 1956," page 5 "Communist Party vs. Subversion Board."
*** See exhibit on page 4.
**** See adjoining illustration.

Frankfurter Quotes Red Propaganda
To Bolster Supreme Court Rulings

(1) Felix Frankfurter used a propaganda-packed Communist Party brief as the basis for his reasons to block attempts to have the Communist apparatus declared "an agency of a foreign power." The below paragraph (in quotes), is from the official Communist Party brief.

Communist Party of the United States of America, Petitioner *v.* Subversive Activities Control Board. [April 30, 1956]	On Writ of Certiorari to the United States Court of Appeals for the District of Columbia Circuit.

MR. JUSTICE FRANKFURTER delivered the opinion of the Court.

Petitioner brought this order to the Court of Appeals for the District of Columbia for review. While the case was pending, it filed a motion, supported by affidavit, for leave to adduce additional evidence pursuant to §14 (a) of the Act.[2] The basis of the motion was that the additional material evidence became available to the petitioner subsequent to the administrative proceeding and that this evidence would "establish that the testimony of three of the witnesses for the Attorney General on which . . . [the Board] relied extensively and heavily in making findings which are of key importance to the order now under review, was false. . . . In summary, this evidence will establish that Crouch, Johnson and Matusow, all professional informers heretofore employed by the Department of Justice as witnesses in numerous proceedings, have committed perjury, are completely untrustworthy and should be accorded no credence; that at least two of them are now being investigated for perjury by the Department of Justice, and that because their character as professional perjurers has now been conclusively and publicly demonstrated, the Attorney General has ceased to employ any of them as witnesses."*

(2) Supreme Court Justice Tom Clark denounced Frankfurter ruling as being "flimsily supported."

MR. JUSTICE CLARK, with whom MR. JUSTICE REED and MR. JUSTICE MINTON join, dissenting.

Believing that the Court here disregards its plain responsibility and duty to decide these important constitutional questions, I cannot join in its action.

I have not found any case in the history of the Court where important constitutional issues have been avoided on such a pretext.

I abhor the use of perjured testimony as much as anyone, but we must recognize that never before have mere allegations of perjury, so flimsily supported, been considered grounds for reopening a proceeding or granting a new trial.**

In at least three cases this Term we declined to review state criminal convictions in which much stronger allegations of perjury were made. See *Reynolds v. Texas*, No. 236; *Whitener v. South Carolina*, No. 218; and *Coco v. Florida*, No. 130.**

---

1. The use of Communist Party political slander material to hand down a ruling in favor of the red conspiracy is typical of Felix Frankfurter.

2. Clark shows that Frankfurter and his cohorts have passed up appeals on regular criminal cases, where the allegations of perjury were well founded, in order to devote time to support the Communist Party allegations which were "flimsily supported." In other words, the reds get special and preferred treatment over all others by the Frankfurter Supreme Court. *(Official published Supreme Court ruling.) **Ibid.

of ability and education and felt himself frustrated by his race and color, and fell under the spell of the communist propaganda.

The Communists, however, reckoned without understanding that the man they had enlisted in their cause had, for them, certain dangerous qualities. He had a Christian upbringing; he was intelligent; and he had courage.

His Christian upbringing made him revolt at the obscene immorality of the Communist Party, and its members.

His intelligence made him see through the stupidity of the communist doctrine, and see that he should strive to be a first class Negro instead of an imitation of a third class white man.

His courage made him willing to confess his sins in public and try to expiate them.

It is for this last quality that the Frankfurter Supreme Court and left-wing press can never forgive him.

I hope you will read Manning Johnson's pamphlet carefully. If you do, you will understand how the communists have used, and are using, certain American Negroes to the detriment of all Americans—white or black.

You will read the story of one Negro who has gone through the fire, and come out tempered steel.

July 22, 1958.   *Archibald B. Roosevelt*

President, THE ALLIANCE, INC.

Chapter One

IN THE WEB

Ten years I labored in the cause of Communism. I was a dedicated "comrade." All my talents and efforts were zealously used to bring about the triumph of Communism in America and throughout the world. To me, the end of capitalism would mark the beginning of an interminable period of plenty, peace, prosperity and universal comradeship. All racial and class differences and conflicts would end forever after the liquidation of the capitalists, their government and their supporters. A world union of Soviet States under the hegemony of Russia would free and lead mankind on to Utopia.

Being an idealist, I was sold this "bill of goods" by a Negro graduate of the Lenin Institute in Moscow.

The color of one's skin is no bar to a young man or woman dreaming of making a better world. Like other Negroes, I experienced and saw many injustices and inequities around me based upon color, not ability. I was told that "the decadent capitalist system is responsible," that "mass pressure" could force concessions but "that just prolongs the life of capitalism"; that I must unite and work with all those who more or less agree that capitalism must go.

Little did I realize until I was deeply enmeshed in the *Red Conspiracy*, that just and seeming grievances are exploited to transform idealism into a cold and ruthless weapon against the capitalist system—that this is the end toward which all the communist efforts among Negroes are directed.

Indeed, I had entered the red conspiracy in the vain belief that it was the way to a "new, better and superior" world system of society. Ten years later, thoroughly disillusioned, I abandoned communism. The experiences of those years in "outer darkness" are like a horrible nightmare. I saw communism in all its naked cruelty, ruthlessness and utter contempt of Christian attributes and passions. And, too, I saw the low value placed upon human life, the total lack of respect for the dignity of man, the betrayal of trust, the terror of the Secret Police and the bloody hand of the assassin, during and since, those fateful years when I embraced communism.

I was lured into the red movement by way of the American Negro Labor Congress, one of the many "front organizations" set up by the communists to trap the naive, unwary, unsuspecting and idealistic Negro. The use of such attractive and appealing fronts as a means of entrapment is a most important serpentine method of the reds.

After two years of practical training in organizing street demonstrations, inciting mob violence, how to fight the police and how to politically "throw a brick and hide", I was ready, in the opinion of my leaders, for a top communist school.

At a secret national training school in New York City, I was given an extensive and intensive course in the theory and practice of red political warfare. As a result, I was appointed District Organizer by the Political Bureau of the Communist Party in the Buffalo, New York area, one of the vital industrial sections of our country. It was in the position of District Organizer that I learned to use secret codes, "mail drops", organize clandestine meetings, "shake police shadows" and other underground activities. At the same time I became acquainted with the nature of communist sabotage and espionage.

My zeal, training, both theoretical and practical, combined with loyalty and willingness to sacrifice, changed me from a novice into a dedicated red—a professional revolutionist. Consequently, I climbed rapidly to the National Committee, the highest governing body of the Communist Party in America.

Being a Negro top communist, I was placed on the National Negro Commission, an important sub-committee of the National Committee of the Communist Party. On this Commission, which was created on direct orders from Moscow to facilitate the subversion of the Negroes, I began to realize the full implications of how the Negro is used as a political dupe by the Kremlin hierarchy. Under the guise of "unity of black and white in the struggle", several top white communists, such as James S. Allen, Elizabeth Lawson, the late Robert "Bob" Minor, and George Blake Charney were placed on the National Negro Commission. These white communists wielded more power than the nominal Negro heads of the Commission. In a word, they are like white overseers. Every Negro member was aware of the fact that these white overseers constituted the eyes, the ears and the voice of the Kremlin. Moreover, these white overseers are the surest functional guarantee of the maintenance of the hierarchial authoritarian control of the Kremlin over their Negro lick spittles directing the conspiracy among Negroes in America.

Indeed, it is the white group on the National Negro Com-

1.

Daily Worker, New York, Wednesday, December 1, 1954

James Jackson's 40th Birthday: Hero Son of the Negro People

By S. D. ROCK

Further, for a period of 15 years he took part in every important general movement for advancement which involved Negro and white labor and progressive forces of the South.

In addition to serving as a founder, vice president and principal organizer of the Southern Negro Youth Congress, he participated in the formation and building of the Southern Conference for Human Welfare, the Southern Regional Council, and many other movements which in any important way challenged the status quo of Negro oppression and Southern social backwardness.

For Communists, Jim Jackson's mastery—though practice—of the united front tactic provides a model of great importance in carrying into life the objectives of the Party program. A primary characteristic of his style of work has been his persistent skill in developing mass struggles around the issues and through the organizational forms and methods closest and most congenial to the masses—all the while striving to raise a given campaign project, or movement to higher levels of social consciousness and fighting capacity, all the while furthering the unity and initiative of Negro and white workers and the leadership of the Negro workers in the Negro liberation movement.

2.

THE WORKER, SUNDAY, JUNE 9, 1957

Seven CP National Secretaries Named

The National Administrative Committee of the Communist Party announced yesterday that its National Executive meeting on May 22-23 elected seven national secretaries.

The seven secretaries are: Benjamin J. Davis, Negro affairs; Eugene Dennis, national affairs; Fred M. Fine, labor affairs; John Gates, public affairs; James E. Jackson, Jr., Southern affairs; Hyman Lumer.

1. James Jackson, a Negro red agent, is used as a symbol among Negro youth, showing that promoting communist front groups with deceptively innocent names is something to boast about. Here Negro reds are told that all racial matters must be bent to fit into the communist mold.

2. In spite of leftist inspired stories "that communism is going out of business in America," the Negro apparatus within the Communist Party has been expanded and is alerted for greater racial agitation. In addition to a "Negro department" a special unit for "Southern Affairs" has been created.

mission that holds full sway. They flatter one or two top Negroes by making them feel they are actually participating in the formulation of policy by consulting with them prior to meetings of the Commission. Then these two Negroes are assigned to lay down the line to the other Negroes on the Commission. The white members check to make sure they do. Their opinion of what a Negro member says at a meeting can either make or break him. Usually, the Negro who is broken is accused of "petty bourgeois nationalism", that is, placing the interests of the Negro above the interests of the Communist Party.

In this connection, I observed how white women communists are used as political prostitutes, cohabiting with high-level Negro communists in order to spy on them. Through such intimate relations, these white women communists are able to elicit information pertaining to family background, sources of income, marital difficulties, arrests, convictions, opinions on communist policy and communist leadership. This information is invaluable to the red hierarchy in their relations with their Negro lickspittles. In top red circles, this is known as "bedroom politics."

White communist women are also used to maneuver top Negro reds into compromising positions that, if revealed, would result in public scandal or disgrace. In this way, the reds make these Negroes permanently subject to blackmail if they ever consider leaving the red movement. Moreover, this information is used to destroy the credibility of the defectee, should he decide to fight the red conspiracy.

The highest position I attained was candidate for the Political Bureau (Politburo) of the Communist Party. The Politburo is a small, close-knit body, carefully selected by the Kremlin hierarchy. Each member holds his position solely on the approval of the reactionary, rapacious despoilers in the Kremlin. This is the real governing body of the entire red conspiracy in America. A candidate is invited to sit in on deliberations with voice but no vote. Usually, a representative of the Kremlin participates in all meetings and deliberations of the Politburo. This writer sat in such meetings when Gerhard Eisler, alias Edwards, Brown, Hans Berger, etc., was the Kremlin representative. Eisler later jumped bail and fled the United States on the red Poish liner "Batory" after he was exposed and convicted of passport fraud.

The assignment of political commissars to the red movement in America is not limited solely to America, but is an established Kremlin policy in relation to all communist parties in countries outside the "Iron Curtain". Kremlin agents, such as Eisler, exercise an awesome power over the white, as well as black lickspittles, comprising the leadership. When Eisler spoke, one could hear a pin fall. Each leader sat in rapt attention, hanging on to every word Eisler uttered as if it were, indeed, a pronouncement from the "Holy of Holies". On several occasions, he expressed the grave dissatisfaction of the Kremlin because of the failure of the party to take advantage of the broad "people's front movement" to build "progressive groups" in participating organizations such as the N.A.A.C.P., youth, religious, fraternal, labor, etc. These "progressive groups", he said, "was the only guarantee that the decisions we make with leaders will be brought down to and carried out by the membership".

Significantly, Eisler emphasized that the "people's front" or "democratic front" is "a maneuver only" to lay the basis for firm communist direction and control of masses. And, too, that the leaders of non-communist organizations are drawn into joint movements with the communists "only to facilitate the infiltration, ideological and organizational penetration of their respective organizations". After all, this is a fight for leadership to determine "who shall lead the masses, the communists or Negro reformists". The "progressive groups", consisting of communists, fellow-travellers, sympathizers, liberals, etc., constitute the vehicle on which the reds pin their present hope of victory.

Never once were we allowed to forget the vacillating, uncertain, untrustworthy character of the Negro intellectual, the Negro minister, the Negro petty bourgeois, the Negro reformist and the white socio-liberal, philanthropic, humanitarian supporter. They are accused, on the basis of experience, of "running frantically from one camp (red) to the other (capitalist) when the going gets tough". So that when communists unite with and support them today, it is necessary to keep in mind that "it may be necessary to denounce them tomorrow and the day after tomorrow hang them".

Thus, as a participant on the highest level of the communist conspiracy in America, I observed the cold, calculating, ruthless nature of red power politics and politcal warfare, stripped of all its illusory propaganda and idealistic cover.

Chapter Two

SUBVERTING NEGRO CHURCHES

Created doubt, lack of confidence, suspicion; setting up situations that bring about racial bitterness, violence and conflict; putting forth demands so unrealistic that race relations are worsened; attacking everybody in disagreement as reactionaries, fascists, Ku Kluxers among whites and Uncle Toms among Negroes, constitute the red's pattern of operation.

Fortunately, the overwhelming majority of Negroes, in whose name the Communists and their ilk presume to speak, have not fallen for the blandishments of the Reds. They know a red light when they see one. The same cannot be said of many Negro intellectuals carrying the ball for Communists. Since the Communists have always looked upon Negro intellectuals as "shallow," "superficial," "phrase-mongers" and "incompetents" "looking for a loaf when they, on a basis of ability, are not worthy of a crumb," their pro-communist behavior becomes all the more tragic and ludicrous.

Only after the order came from Moscow in the 1934-35 period to win over the Negro intellectual by deceptive flattery and adulation did the red's public attitude toward them change. The Kremlin concluded that these "superficial phonies" could serve the cause of Communism.

A large number of Negro ministers are all for the Communists. Some are prominent and influential; others are "run of the mill." They in common believe that beating the racial drums is a short cut to prominence, money and the realization of personal ambitions even if the Negro masses are left prostrate and bleeding—expendables in the mad scramble for power.

Abner W. Berry, columnist in *The Daily Worker*, official organ of the Communist Party, recently praised these ministers as fulfilling their "historic role," i.e., delivering the Negro into the hands of the Communists. Neither his pen nor his lips had such praise prior to the 1934-35 period. Then the Moscow line was clear.

The resolution on the Negro Question stated:

"In the work among the Negroes, special attention should be paid to the role played by the churches and preachers who are acting on behalf of American imperialism. The Party must conduct a continuous and carefully worked out campaign among the Negro masses, sharpened primarily against the preachers and the churchmen, who are the agents of the oppressors of the Negro race."*

All the instructions from Moscow at the time ordered reds to "combat the influence of the church" because the church, "by offering to the Negro worker and peasant for the miseries they are enduring in this world, compensation in heaven, are befogging the minds of the Negro workers and peasants, making them a helpless prey to capitalism and imperialism."**

The public denunciation of Negro "sky pilots"*** was likewise stopped on orders from Moscow. The deeply re-

---

* *Political Secretariat, Communist International*, Moscow, U.S.S.R. *Resolution on Negro Question in U.S.*
** Issued by International Trade Union Committee of Negro Workers of R.I.L.U (Red International of Labor Unions.)
*** A cynical Communist name for the clergy.

ligious Negro masses whom the Kremlin wanted to use as expendables in the struggle for power shied away from the "Party." A frontal attack on religion resulted in isolation from Negroes. Therefore, deception was to be tried. The honeyed phrase replaced harsh words. The smile replaced the smirk. The velvet glove covered the mailed fist. Humility replaced arrogance. The handshake replaced hostility. All that was distasteful and wicked in the past was to be forgotten in the face of "a need for a common front against the white oppressors." *The devil was sick—an angel he would be.*

Application of the new line embarked the Communists on an era of outstanding success in infiltrating and penetrating the Negro Church.

White ministers acting as missionaries, using the race angle as bait, aided in the cultivation of Negro ministers for work in the Red solar system of organizations. Bribery through gifts, paid lectures, flattery through long applause at staged rallies, favorable mention in the red controlled press were not the only methods employed to corrupt the Negro ministers. The use of sex and perversion as a means of political blackmail was an accepted red tactic.

At the same time that all this was going on at the top, the "comrades" were building cells below in the church "to guarantee that decisions made at the top would be brought down to the congregation."

The importance attached to this work is clearly shown in the report of the speeches of Earl Browder, then General Secretary of the Communist Party, and Gerhard Eisler, alias Edwards, Moscow representative to the plenary session of the National Committee of the Communist Party in the United States. It states:

[15]

"Comrades Browder, Edwards and Ford have spoken about the necessity of making a turn in our Negro work . . . how to connect ourselves with the organized masses . . . in the United States there are . . . of the Negro population . . . 10 million in churches. The problem of how to penetrate these organizations is of the utmost political importance."*

The bulk of Negro church members are in the South. They live by the "Good Book." Anyone against the "Good Book" is of the devil. There is no *in between*. The Red carpet-baggers discovered this when they touched the Negro's religion. So they avoided this sore spot in order to snare their intended victims. Get them involved in the movement first and later do the job on their religious convictions was the order. Anything else was putting the cart before the horse.

The new line went like this: Jesus, the carpenter, was a worker like the Communists. He was against the "money changers," the "capitalists," the "exploiters" of that day. That is why he drove them from the temple. The Communists are the modern day fighters against the capitalists or money changers. If Jesus were living today, he would be persecuted like the Communists who seek to do good for the common people.

Alert law enforcement agents made it extremely difficult and hazardous for the Reds to work openly. Consequently, they drew heavily upon the accumulated knowledge and experience of their comrades engaged in illegal work in other parts of the world to operate with the least risk in the South. Of all their methods used, it was generally agreed that the Church is the "best cover for illegal work."

Party Organizer, March, 1935. page 16, Issued by the Central Committee Communist Party.

Gilbert Green, one of the top Reds in this country, reported as follows:

"For example in the South we have more than 300 members who are also members of church youth organizations — especially the Baptist Young Peoples Union. In this district (Alabama) . . . where possible we should build . . . units in the Church Youth organizations. Why? Because in the South, especially for the Negro youth, the church is the center of cultural and social activity. It is here that we must work. By building our units in the church organizations we can also improve our work under the illegal conditions, as it will be easier to work in the church organizations. In Alabama there are certain places in which we can in a short while take over the church organizations of youth, under our leadership, and these can become *legal covers for our work in the South.* (Italics mine.) *

* Excerpt Report of Gil Green for the National Bureau to a meeting of the Enlarged National Executive Committee, held in New York on February 23, 1935. *Int. of Youth*, March, 1935, pages 25, 26.

Chapter Three

RED PLOT TO USE NEGROES

Stirring up race and class conflict is the basis of all discussion of the Communist Party's work in the South. The evil genius, Stalin, and the other megalomaniacal leaders in Moscow ordered the use of all racial, economic and social differences, no matter how small or insignificant, to start local fires of discontent, conflict and revolt. "Who could tell which of these issues could start a general conflagration" that would sweep across the former Confederate States from Maryland to Texas?

Black rebellion was what Moscow wanted. Bloody racial conflict would split America. During the confusion, demoralization and panic would set in. Then finally, the reds say:

> "Workers stop work, many of them seize arms by attacking arsenals. Many had armed themselves before ... Street fights become frequent. Under the leadership of the Communist Party the workers organize Revolutionary Committees to be in command of the uprising. Armed workers ... seize the principal government offices, invade the residences of the President and his Cabinet members, arrest them, declare the old regime abolished, establish their own power. . . ."*

---

* *Why Communism?*, by M. J. Olgin, pages 75, 76. (Official Communist pamphlet instructing members in revolutionary strategy.)

The only fear of the white Communist leaders was that as a result of their efforts this black rebellion would break out before they were ready in the decisive industrial cities of the North.

What if one or five million Negroes die in an abortive attempt to establish a Negro republic? Is not the advance of the cause worth it? A Communist is not a sentimentalist. He does not grieve over the loss of life in the advancement of Communism.

This plot to use the Negroes as the spearhead, or as expendables, was concocted by Stalin in 1928, nearly ten years after the formation of the world organization of Communism. Prior to this time, the periodic Moscow gatherings did little more than pass resolutions. Any credit for the change belongs, in the main, to a handful of Negro lickspittles like James W. Ford, Harry Haywood, Otto Hall, Lovett Fort-Whiteman, and Otto Huiswood, to mention a few.

They were the ones who, again and again, begged their masters in Moscow to force the white leaders of the Communist Party in the United States to organize and use the Negroes. They were the ones who got in on the ground floor of the conspiracy. They are the ones that history may well record as the political Uncle Toms who plotted with a diabolical alien power the moral decay, physical slavery and spiritual death of their own race.

The perfidy of these Negro Reds is all the more infamous when one reads from the pen of a top Negro Communist who wrote:

(a) "Prior to the Sixth Congress, white chauvinism (race prejudice) . . . made progress in Negro work well-nigh impossible;

(b) "White chauvinism manifests itself . . . in open or concealed opposition to doing work among Negroes;

(c) "The tendency . . . was to ignore the leading Negro comrades when formulating policy;

(d) "As punishment for their opposition . . . the Negro comrades were refused support (financial) in getting out the weekly news service which was being sent out to some three hundred Negro newspapers;

(e) "Negro comrade was disciplined for his insistence in bringing before the Conference the tabooed question of Negro work."*

The above red author gives James W. Ford credit for bringing this matter to the attention of the *White Fathers* in Moscow which resulted in immediate action. Negro communists were given jobs in the apparatus. Most of them were given professional revolutionary training in the United States and Russia under direct orders from Stalin. As a result, Negro reds began looking to Moscow. Stalin became the great and just *"Father"* who could be relied upon to settle the many differences between white and Negro communists.

During the three decades which have elapsed since the Sixth World Congress in Moscow, the American Communist Party has conducted many campaigns and formed and infiltrated a large number of organizations among Negroes. From the bloody gun battles at Camp Hill, Alabama (1931), to the present integration madness, the heavy hand of communism has moved, stirring up racial strife, creating confusion, hate and bitterness so essential to the advancement of the red cause.

---

* *Our Negro Work,* by Cyril Briggs, *The Communist,* Sept., 1929.

America Was Alerted Over 25 Years Ago
Red Plans for Race War Went Unheeded

(1) In 1926 R. M. Whitney wrote a book which exposed the red plot in all its major ramifications. It was profusely illustrated with documents seized from communist sources by Federal authorities.

The most colossal conspiracy against the United States in its history was unearthed at Bridgman, Michigan, August 22, 1922, when the secret Convention of the Communist Party of America was raided by the Michigan Constabulary, aided by county and Federal officials. Two barrels full of documentary proof of the conspiracy were seized and are in possession of the authorities. Names, records, checks from prominent people in this country, instructions from Moscow, speeches, theses, questionnaires—indeed, the whole machinery of the underground organization, the avowed aim of which is the overthrow of the United States Government, was found in such shape as to condemn every participant in the convention.

It is now known and can be made public to what extent this movement, inspired from Moscow and directed by Lenin and Trotsky, has grown since the first seeds were sown a few years ago.

(2) The following racial program was read to a meeting of assembled communist leaders in Bridgman, Michigan on August 20, 1922. The reds proceeded with this program, in spite of exposure, and have accomplished practically all of their objectives. Today we see the tragic effects of public and official indifference.

"In order that the Negro may be reached with education and propaganda and that he may be organized for activity, the following methods are recommended:

"1.—Nuclei shall be established in all existing Negro organizations, such as fraternal, religious and labor organizations, cooperatives, tenant farmers' leagues, etc.

"2.—Colored organizers and speakers shall be sent among Negroes in order to inform them and win their confidence.

"3.—Newspapers and publications shall be established or, when this is not feasible, news service shall be established by friendly cooperation with colored newspapers of liberal tenets.

"4.—Friendship of liberal-minded Negro ministers shall be sought as these men are at the present time the leaders of the Negro masses and many of them are earnest but lack scientific knowledge.

"5.—Conferences on the economic conditions among Negroes shall be held from time to time with these ministers, educators and other liberal elements, and through their influence the party shall aim to secure a more favorable hearing before the Negro masses.

"6.—By means of its membership the party shall penetrate the existing forums, literary societies, lyceums, schools, colleges, teachers' institutes, etc., of the colored people, and establish forums of its own for the enlightenment of the Negro population.

"7—Where other forms of activity are impossible or impracticable as in certain Southern districts, cooperatives may be formed."*

*Reference—Reds in America by R. M. Whitney, page 193, published by Beckwith Press, Inc., New York City, 1926.

One may recall organizations formed, directed, controlled and led by Reds and fellow travellers such as: American Negro Labor Congress, League of Struggle for Negro Rights, International Labor Defense, National Negro Congress, Sharecroppers Union, the Civil Rights Congress, Negro Labor Victory Committee, Southern Negro Youth Congress, Negro Labor Councils, etc., ad infinitum, that exposed millions of Negroes to Communist ideas.

The list of sponsors, officers, and contributors reads like a Who's Who in the Negro intellectual, professional, labor and religious circles.

Through the aforementioned organizations and many others, Negro institutions of higher education like Howard University were penetrated to subvert teachers and students and thus politically contaminate the intellectual stream of Negro life.

White leftists descended on Negro communities like locusts, posing as "friends" come to help "liberate" their black brothers. Along with these white communist missionaries came the Negro political Uncle Toms to allay the Negro's distrust and fears of these strangers. Everything was inter-racial, an inter-racialism artificially created, cleverly devised as a camouflage of the red plot to use the Negro.

Chapter Four

BANE OF RED INTEGRATION

Many Negro intellectuals, artists, professionals, etc., were carried away with this outburst of inter-racialism. Here was an opportunity to be accepted by the other racial group. Secretly, they had always wanted to get away from the other Negroes. Moving around among whites would somehow add to their stature and endow a feeling of importance. So they went after communist inter-racialism like a hog going after slop.

There are numerous examples of the harmful and deadening effect of communist inter-racialism (integration) on any proposal for constructive Negro projects. Of these examples, I will cite only a few.

First, during the latter 1930's, the Negro and white reds, fellow travelers, et al., waged an intense campaign against Harlem Hospital in New York. Inside information, supplied by reds on the hospital staff, told of crowded conditions and improper treatment. Some of this information was so derogatory that many dubbed Harlem Hospital the "Butcher Shop." Street meetings, indoor rallies, united front conferences made overcrowding and improper hospital treatment the main subject matter. Demands were made on the city officials for more and better hospitals without success. Charges of race discrimination filled the air. The reds had a field day building up racial tensions.

Everybody was talking about the overcrowding in the Harlem Hospital. So a group of Negroes, believing in "doing something for yourself," came up with the idea of a Negro community effort to found a hospital. They saw in such a project a chance to render great service to the people in the community and to show to the Nation and the world an example of Negro resourcefulness. Jews, Catholics, Presbyterians and others founded hospitals, so why not Negroes?

The Communists were not interested in a Negro hospital, founded by Negroes and redounding to their credit. Such a project would take away a key issue in racial agitation and radicalization and isolate the reds. So they acted swiftly and decisively, through their Negro intellectual tools in the community, to kill the project aborning.

The late Claude McKay, Negro poet, whom I knew very well, wrote about it as follows:

"There was a project to found a Negro hospital a few years ago, but before it was launched the idea was killed by the obstreperous and extremely vocal and effective group of Negro intellectuals who style themselves the 'anti-Segregationists'. They maintained that a Negro hospital would be an incentive to the greater segregation of Negro doctors.

"Preposterous is the situation in which the entire Negro minority is placed by its irrational intellectuals and their canny 'radical' white supporters.

"I predict that nothing could be more effective in breaking down the barriers of Segregation and compelling white doctors to recognize the merits of colored colleagues than the establishment of a great Negro hospital in Harlem. . . . Moreover, such an institution could become an asset to the American medical profession. White doctors would be more attracted by the outstanding work of their colored colleagues, just as white educators and intellectuals were drawn to Tuskegee to study the great work of Booker T. Washington."*

Second. A well-known Negro real estate man called together a group of prominent Negro intellectuals and professionals for the purpose of launching a Negro housing development through the purchase of land and home construction. Such a project, he argued, would go a long way in showing other races that Negroes can build ideal communities and maintain standards second to none. He had maps showing fine locations that even from a land purchase angle proved that it was a good investment. But he couldn't get to first base. Why? Because they were against setting up "Negro Communities," that is "segregating ourselves." "They," he said, "were all for integration in white communities."

Third. A prominent Negro dentist, who became "well to do" in the Negro community, takes great pride in his radical views and associations. He purchased a home in a "White Neighborhood" for $20,000. He has since added approximately $10,000 for repairs and alterations. Publicly, he boasted about his being the only Negro family in the neighborhood. He makes his money off Negroes; he is a Negro; but he doesn't want to live among them. To him, the mark of success is a good bank reserve and a home in a white neighborhood. His only fear is that his white neighbors will sell to other Negroes and move to another area. To him, and to so many others of his ilk, the very thought of members of his own race replacing his newly found white neighbors gives him "conniptions."

---

* *Harlem: Negro Metropolis*, by Claude McKay, page 124, pub. 1940.

An Editorial

By His Own Admission

Arkansas Gazette.
LITTLE ROCK
ARKANSAS

June 20, 1958

OFFICE OF THE
EDITOR

Dear Mr. Loeb:

Your most recent letter convinces me that if you are not in fact unaware of the editorial position of the Gazette, you are quite willing to distort it for your own purposes.

However, be that as it may, I have no objection to answering the questions you asked.

We do not at this time have any Negro editorial employe on the Gazette, although in the past we have had such employes on a part-time basis. There is no policy prohibition against hiring Negroes, but we see no particular need for one now and recognize that any Negro staff member would operate under considerable restrictions due to the prevailing mores and customs of the community.

Of course we segregate Negro obituary notices as we segregate advertisements in the classified section dealing with Negro real estate. It has also long been our policy and will continue to be to identify persons in all news stories by race

Sincerely,

Harry S. Ashmore
Executive Editor

Mr. William Loeb
Manchester Union Leader
Manchester, New Hampshire

HARRY S. ASHMORE, executive editor of the Arkansas Gazette, who recently won a Pulitzer Prize for his "crusading" editorials against segregation during the Little Rock crisis, reveals in the above letter that although he believes integration to be fine for Central High School, it is not so fine for the Gazette. ✳✳

✳ Displayed on the front page of the Manchester Union Leader, June 28, 1958. Reproduced by special permission of Mr. William Loeb, publisher of the Manchester Union Leader, Manchester, New Hampshire.

However, it makes no difference what are the circumstances. The Negro crasher of the "Lily White Section" is sure of full cooperation and aid of the reds and all so-called progressives to beat down and discredit the opposition.

Negro integrationists, in the main, can be placed in three groups, as follows:

(a) Those who seek acceptance in white communities only for themselves, to the complete exclusion of other Negroes.

(b) Those who are paid agents of unprincipled or racketeering white real estate men, exploiting the anxieties and fears of the white community to reap a financial bonanza.

(c) Those who are block busters, that is a Negro family for whom the reds or so-called progressives have either purchased or rented a home or an apartment with the full knowledge that its transfer is going to arouse social resentment, bitterness and hostility.

Regardless of the group into which the Negro integrationist falls, he is like "manna from Heaven" to all those who deliberately seek to arrest the steady advancement in race relations and to turn it into a shambles for alien or partisan political purposes.

Significant it is to note that the reds and so-called progressives never spend money on projects to "help" the Negroes unless these projects pay off in race conflict and animosity. They know that the "blockbuster," like the interloper and party crasher, is always resented and usually gets the "bum's rush." That is why they seek to cast the Negro in such a light. It builds up open and hidden resentment that can be exploited.

Some people describe New York City as a "melting pot." At best, this is only wishful thinking. The numerous racial and national groups are as easily identified today as ever. The geographical areas where each group settled or resettled remains. Thus, there are in New York German sections, Italian sections, Irish sections, Jewish sections, Puerto Rican sections, Chinese sections, Negro sections, etc. In short, there may be found as many sections as there are national groups or races. National, social, cultural, linguistic, religious and other common factors effect this sectional cleavage. Parades and gala affairs in national costumes are not uncommon. The same may be said of every part of our country. Though these national, racial and religious differences divide them like five fingers on the hand, yet they are one solid fist as Americans.

The Communists try to exploit these national, racial and religious differences in order to weaken, undermine and subjugate America to Moscow. Like a serpent, they use guile to seduce each group. At no time have the Communists even hinted or suggested to any group, other than the Negro, that their clannishness or tendency to colonize a given area creates a "Ghetto" or "Quarters." Were they to do so, they would be jeered out of each section as crackpots.

Evidently the reds had international propaganda in mind when they described Negro sections as "Ghettos" because the definition of the word *Ghetto* in no way applies to a Negro section any more than it does to a German, Irish, Jewish, Chinese or any other section in America.

The *Encyclopedia Britannica* states:

"Ghetto, formerly the street or quarter of a city in which Jews were compelled to live, enclosed by walls and gates which were locked each night. The term is now used loosely of any locality in a city or country where Jews congregate.

"During the Middle Ages the Jews were forbidden to leave the ghetto after sunset when the gates were locked, and they were also imprisoned on Sundays and all Christian holy days."*

Negroes band together in sections like other races and national groups much for the same reasons. Like other racial and national groups, they can buy land, build communities, settle in any section of the country. Like other racial and national groups, they can make their sections as nice and attractive as possible. The maximum business, cultural, sanitary and social services are within their reach as with other groups.

The Communists, through propaganda, have sold a number of Negro intellectuals the idea that the Negro section is a ghetto; that white Americans created it, set its geographical boundaries; that it is the product of race hate and the inhumanity of white Americans. Therefore, it is a struggle of Negro against "white oppressors" for emancipation.

Naturally, those holding such views have no community pride, no interest in doing anything to improve its services because that would be aiding and abetting "segregation" and maintenance of the "ghetto."

Moreover, they oppose any race project inside or outside the Negro section for the same reason. Everything has to be integrated or it is *taboo*. In this way, they paralyze Negro initiative and resourcefulness, casting the race in the mold of one that is incapable of producing anything for the advancement of society. At the same time, it creates

* *The Encyclopedia Britannica*, XI Edition, pages 920-921.

the impression among other racial groups that the Negro waits for them to prepare the banquet so that he can step in and enjoy it.

Obviously, this line, deliberately spread by the Communists, leads to the worst kind of mischief. It strengthens and creates racial prejudices and lays the basis for sharp racial conflicts. Shirking social responsibility and blaming others may be the easy way, but it is only a short cut to Communist slavery.

Chapter Five

DESTROYING THE OPPOSITION

No small amount of support of the Communist cause came from important and influential Negro newspapers. The late Robert Minor, a top Red, wrote:

"In some of these papers repeatedly appear open admissions that the Communist Party is the only party that advocates or fights for equal rights for Negroes and the right of self-determination for the Negro people."*

He cited two of "many examples" of this reaction of the Negro press. Because of lack of space, I shall quote only three excerpts from one of his examples:

"No Menacing Reds (From *The Afro-American,* Baltimore).

"The Reds are going our way. Like ourselves, they represent a feared and hated cause. They are the first white group since Emancipation to advocate race, social equality and intermarriage for those who wish it.

"In fact, there is more real Christianity among white Communists than in the white Y.M.C.A., the white Christian Endeavor Societies, or the white so-called Christian Churches.

"The Reds are no menace to Negroes. In fact, it is comforting to find groups of such people as Communists in this color mad world."**

---

* *The Negro and His Judases,* by Robert Minor, *The Communist,* July, 1931, page 634.
** *Ibid.*

There were also Negro intellectuals, artists, professionals, politicians, etc., seeking a ladder to success. They are used according to the strategic needs of the Communist Party. In preparation for their treacherous role, the Party passes along the word covertly or openly to give them preferred treatment. Forces, money, publicity, etc., are used in the build-up to change comparative Negro unknowns into national and international "Race Leaders."

Wires were pulled in local, state and federal governments to appoint, upgrade and transfer to strategic positions Negroes whom the communist apparatus could use. Congressional records show that an internationally prominent Negro was aided in his rise by red spy, Alger Hiss. We have never heard of this same Negro ever recommending any qualified member of his own race as a government appointee. The record does show that he recommended white appointees, later shown to be connected with the Communist conspiracy.

Take also the example of a well-known Negro Federal judge who made two rulings in favor of the criminal communist conspiracy. He was known as a communist fronter before he was appointed. He is hailed in the Red press and was boomed for the Supreme Court.

In both instances, the long range investment of the Communists paid off. Similar examples can be cited again and again. As a result, belief has grown among Negro opportunists that if you want to get ahead, play ball with the reds.

Whenever the reds do a successful "job" on a so-called renegade or militant anti-Communist, it rivets tighter the "conspiratorial cover" of the Party. To insure this end, nothing is more enlightening than a few object lessons.

The awesome spectacle of the array of forces in all walks of life, potent and with ample money, cold-bloodedly and efficiently going about the job of destroying the reputation and influence of those designated as enemies of Communism keep many in line and enforce silence.

And, too, the hand of the assassin is used in some instances where it can be done with impunity.

Few men want the medicine the reds gave the late Senator Joseph McCarthy which the reds boast is the best cure for militant anti-Communists.

Also among those at the top of the list of red victims are George Hewitt, alias Timothy "Tim" Holmes, William "Bill" Nowell and Charles White (murdered). They were Negro professional revolutionists having received their training in the Lenin Institute in Moscow, U.S.S.R. Years of experience on all levels of the Communist apparatus eminently qualified them for the task of ripping the conspiratorial cover from the Communist Party and exposing the flagitious plot against the Negro. When these Negroes defected, they automatically became a serious threat to the Party. Their knowledge of the inner workings of the conspiracy made them a danger to the red apparatus because they were beyond its power of discipline. Theirs was a sincere and total abandonment of Communism. They knew of their own knowledge its dire threat to humanity, so they cooperated with all government agencies investigating, exposing and prosecuting Communists. As a result, they became "enemies of the Party apparatus," "renegades of Communism" and were treated like outcasts with every Red Hand against them.

The National Disciplinary Commission of the Communist Party, feared and respected by all reds, as an arm of the

Soviet Secret Police, placed on these defecters the word "informer,"* the dreaded tag of the criminal underworld. This solemn pronouncement means the "full treatment" to show the "comrades" what happens to those who desert and fight the Party. So complete was the campaign of slander, threats, persecution, social ostracism that all the above-mentioned Negro ex-reds were driven to an untimely grave.

That this can happen in our Republic under God is unbelievable but *TRUE*. No wonder then that today the wrath of the Communists is more to be feared than the Judgments of Heaven.

To sink their claws in, subvert and use the Negro people, Moscow must have loyal, dedicated, trained Negro professional revolutionists who can easily be manipulated, that is, made to follow the Party line.

Loyalty is placed first because the Communist Party leaders demand that loyalty to the Party be placed above and before *everything* and that includes race, relatives, family and loved ones. It entails a complete surrender of the will to the communist hierarchy. A willingness to do anything, go anywhere and say anything you are told is a condition of communist membership.

Out of the fires of such exacting indoctrination and training have come the treacherous Negro red leaders who serve faithfully their masters in the Kremlin. The James Jacksons, the Henry Winstons, the William Pattersons, the Louise Thompsons, the Maude Whites, the Harry Haywoods, the Ben Davises, the Doxey Wilkersons, the James W. Fords, et al., make up the cadre around which the present racial conflict or "liberation movement" is being built.

* See page 4, the "Frankfurter" opinion.

Moreover, they are the ones who devise the methods and techniques used by their puppets to destroy the reputation and influence of those who stand in the way of the gathering momentum of the Negro liberation juggernaut.

Except for a brief period during the latter 1930's, the reds called those persons "Uncle Toms" who sought solution of the race problem through the medium of education, patience, understanding and discussion which would lead to mutual agreement. Since any program leading to a peaceful solution of the race problem automatically excludes and dooms red efforts among Negroes, it goes without saying that the reds are going to oppose it. The chief targets are the responsible advocates of such a program. They must "be discredited and isolated from the masses." So, in addition to the tags of "enemy of the race," "tool of the white ruling class," "traitor to the race," the reds have added the opprobrium of *"Uncle Tom."*

In their usual diabolically clever way, the reds took the name of a fine, sincere and beloved character made famous in the greatest indictment of chattel slavery and transformed him into a "dirty, low, sneaky, treacherous, groveling, snivering coward." This the reds did in order to make the name *"Uncle Tom"* the symbol of social, economic and political leprosy.

Today, the name *"Uncle Tom"* among Negroes ranks with the term *"McCarthyism"* generally, turning many ministers into moral cowards, many politicians into scared jackrabbits and many other leaders in hypocrites.

No man dare stand up and proclaim convictions counter to red agitation without running the certain risk of being pilloried. The reds, their fellow travelers, leaders of the

N.A.A.C.P. and other race agitators have created an ideal climate for such persecution.

Ironically, the communist definition of *"Uncle Tom"* applies to the Negro red and fellow traveler more than it does to any one else. In fact, I do not know of any Negro, living or dead, who sank to the depths of cowardice, servility, and treachery as has the Negro red. One has only to read the "wailings and lamentations" of Pettis Perry to his white masters in the Communist Party to do something about the widespread race prejudice permeating that Party from top to bottom. Such prejudice in the Communist Party, in the opinion of Pettis Perry, prevents the communist apparatus from effectively exploiting the Negro people.

Chapter Six

THE REAL "UNCLE TOMS"

Ironically, after more than three decades, the reds can't eliminate race prejudice from their own ranks. Pettis Perry's articles clearly show that the centuries' old racial, national, social, economic and political differences between peoples plague and bedevil the communist vanguard despite indoctrination, training, discipline and so forth. The human element resists the red straitjacket.

Naturally so, because you can't level everybody off, toss them in a pot, and stir them up without producing a social disorder.

The top white Communist leaders know that racial, as well as other differences between peoples, have existed over a long span of years and will continue to exist even after centuries of re-education under Communist rule. They also know that these differences can be used to play race against race, nationality against nationality, class against class, etc., to advance the cause of Communism.

Posing as a "friend of the Negro," they, under the guise of a campaign for Negro rights, set race against race in the cold-blooded struggle for power. Their hypocrisy and the falsity of their claims are clearly revealed in a number of instances.

[37]

For example, while the reds and their fellow travelers were stoking the racial fires on the issue of restrictive covenants:

"In New York, some 46 comrades, including the chairman, signed leases containing restrictive covenant clauses. This was also true of two leading comrades in the trade union movement. . . . Some comrades said 'that those involved needed a home' and therefore . . . it was 'all right' for them to sign such clauses."*

While the white reds were renting apartments and subletting them to Negroes to stir up racial bitterness and hate such as existed in Stuyvesant Town, in New York City, they carefully avoided living in a Negro community. A top white red "was in the act of moving in to the Riverton Housing Project in Harlem, but decided against it because," to quote him, "a survey disclosed that only 5 to 7 per cent of the inhabitants of the project were white families, and therefore that would have been a bad environment for my kids."**

The white Communists have nothing but contempt for Negro Communists (and justly so) and this is openly expressed. For instance:

"White comrades living in a Negro community and holding positions in the clubs were not on speaking terms with most of the Negro comrades.***

Their utter hypocrisy is also revealed in the following:

"White comrades going into the mass organizations made up predominantly of Negro people . . . constant-

---

* *Political Affairs*, June, 1949, Article by Pettis Perry, pages 3-12.
** *Ibid.*
*** *Ibid.*

ly shout that 'We must fight for Negro rights.' Yet when they meet Negro comrades and other Negro acquaintances on the street, especially in the downtown area, they do not even speak to them."*

Evidently, fear and distrust of the Negro male is rampant in Communist Party ranks because when the

" . . . newspapers reported a case of rape, some of the white women in the Party began to develop the idea that they should ask for police 'protection'."**

Even the despised "tools of the capitalist system" (the police) are good to have around at times, say the comrades.

From time to time, the Communist leaders conduct a complete registration of all members. Any Negro comrade who does not register is told to do so or else. The "else" means loss of job as for instance:

"In New Jersey, there was difficulty in . . . re-registering a Negro woman comrade, whereupon this comrade was informed that either she re-register 'or else it will be your job',"

thus implying

"that the Party would use its influence to carry out the threat."***

Social equality for the Negro is a major slogan of the Communists. They use it on the one hand to mislead the Negro American, and on the other hand to create anxieties and fears among white Americans to better exploit both racial groups. What it means when applied to the Communist is shown as follows:

---

* *Political Affairs*, June, 1949 (Official Organ of the Communist Party), article by Pettis Perry, pages 3-12.
** *Ibid.*
*** *Ibid.*

1. National Guardian Second Five-Year Plan in Crisis

WHY INDIA STILL SUFFERS FROM POVERTY AND MISERY

By Tabitha Petran
Guardian Staff Correspondent

NEW DELHI, INDIA

INDIA'S MOOD appears to be one of cynicism and disillusion. In ten years of independence and five years of planning the common man's lot has improved little.

The "hope level" to which Prime Minister Nehru refers is sinking rapidly with further emasculation of the plan. It is difficult to find the reality behind India's "democratic way to socialism" which, Nehru says, is distinguished by respect for the "dignity of man."

LIVING CONDITIONS: For example, at night thousands of Indians sleep on the pavements of the streets of Calcutta and Bombay. To many millions in villages and cities, streets, store fronts, verandahs provide the only "home" they ever know. Millions live in worse than slums.

In Bombay's Matunga Colony some 20,000 are crowded into tiny shacks of mud, tin, boards or thatch, 8 to 16 in a room inch deep in garbage and (during the monsoon) in mud, lacking drainage and even latrines. A million live in Calcutta's "bustees"—long sheds divided into windowless cells, 8 to 25 in a room.

KENNELS FOR PEOPLE: "One of the best" bustees I visited had two drinking water taps and 32 latrines for 2,000 people. Outside Poona, people crawl into what look like oversized dog kennels in which they cannot stand up.

With per capita food consumption lower than before the war, whole regions of India still suffer from chronic famine and people eat leaves and grass during lean periods.

---

1. Rev. Martin Luther King, Negro leader of the Montgomery, Alabama, racial disturbances, along with a host of leftist agitators, has been trying to sell India and its "passive resistance" theory as an ideal to be followed by American Negroes. The *National Guardian*, a pro-Soviet paper, pictures millions of East Indians as living in a condition of almost incredible poverty and degradation.*

*The *National Guardian* was cited by a Congressional body as "a virtual official propaganda arm of Soviet Russia." (Committee on Un-American Activities, House Report 3123, September 21, 1950.)

"A number of instances . . . Negro comrades are not welcome into the homes of white comrades. In some cases, they are received early in the morning, when neighbors may think they are domestic workers, or are welcome at night, when the neighbors of the white comrades might not see the Negro comrades at all."*

Space does not permit the citing of all the many examples of the utter hypocrisy of the white Communists which show the vast gulf between what they say and what they do.

* *Political Affairs*, June, 1949.

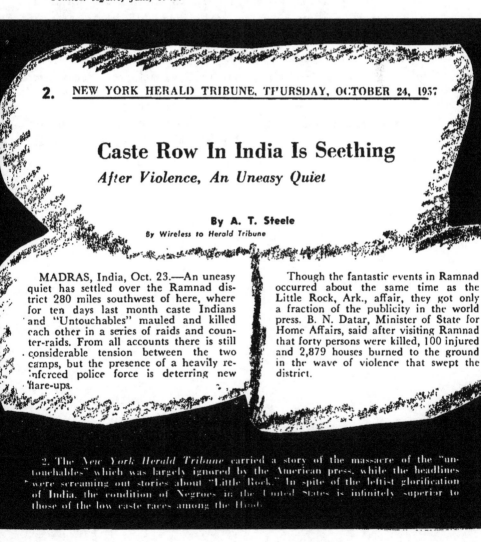

Caste Row In India Is Seething

After Violence, An Uneasy Quiet

By A. T. Steele

By Wireless to Herald Tribune

MADRAS, India, Oct. 23.—An uneasy quiet has settled over the Ramnad district 280 miles southwest of here, where for ten days last month caste Indians and "Untouchables" mauled and killed each other in a series of raids and counter-raids. From all accounts there is still considerable tension between the two camps, but the presence of a heavily reinforced police force is deterring new flare-ups.

Though the fantastic events in Ramnad occurred about the same time as the Little Rock, Ark., affair, they got only a fraction of the publicity in the world press. B. N. Datar, Minister of State for Home Affairs, said after visiting Ramnad that forty persons were killed, 100 injured and 2,879 houses burned to the ground in the wave of violence that swept the district.

2. The *New York Herald Tribune* carried a story of the massacre of the "untouchables" which was largely ignored by the American press, while the headlines were screaming out stories about "Little Rock." In spite of the leftist glorification of India, the condition of Negroes in the United States is infinitely superior to those of the low caste races among the Hindu.

These examples serve to bring into sharp focus the infamous treachery of the Negro reds and their Negro fellow travelers and defenders. Moreover, it conjures up their own definition of *"Uncle Tom"* which applies more to them than to any other Negro.

The reds have deliberately twisted and warped the thinking of those intellectual pygmies who lead the "Freedom by '63" campaign by sending them after quick solutions of a centuries' old problem that has never been solved anywhere in the world. Obvious even to the most ignorant is the fact that all people are prejudiced. No one is free of it. Prejudice, in one form or another, has existed almost as long as the human family. They arise out of the complex differences of race, nationality, religion, economic, social and cultural standing.

Prejudice is not limited to any one race. It is common to all. Neither does the color of skin determine more or less the extent of prejudice in any particular race.

Chapter Seven

CREATING HATE

The red propagandists distort the facts concerning racial differences for ulterior motives. All the *right* is not on the Negro side. Neither is all wrong. The same holds true with regard to the white man's side. The repository of good or evil is not to be found in any particular race. Black men are just as good or as bad as white men. Yellow men are just as good or as bad as brown or red. It ill behooves anyone to speak about the other.

White men sold white men as slaves. Black men sold black men as slaves. Black rulers are no more humane than yellow, red or white rulers. Neither are they less brutal.

The placing of the repository of everything, right and just, among the darker races is a dastardly Communist trick to use race as a means of grabbing and enslaving the whole of humanity.

Moscow's Negro tools in the incitement of racial warfare place all the ills of the Negro at the door of the white leaders of America. Capitalism and imperialism are made symbols of oppressive white rule in keeping with instructions from the Kremlin.

To one familiar with red trickery, it is obvious that placing the blame for all the Negroes' ills at the door of the white leaders in America is to remove all responsibility from the Negro. This tends to make the Negro:

(a) feel sorry for himself;

(b) blame others for his failures;

(c) ignore the countless opportunities around him;

(d) jealous of the progress of other racial and national groups;

(e) expect the white man to do everything for him;

(f) look for easy and quick solutions as a substitute for the harsh realities of competitive struggle to get ahead.

The result is a persecution complex—a warped belief that the white man's prejudices, the white man's system, the white man's government is responsible for everything. Such a belief is the way the reds plan it, for the next logical step is hate that can be used by the reds to accomplish their ends.

In their campaign against the white leaders in America, the reds are careful to point out that this does not apply to the white leaders of Russia and their counterparts in America. This creates the illusion that the white communists are different; that they are the friends and champions of the Negroes. This is the same sucker bait the reds used to win and use millions of white peoples now under the whiplash of Soviet tyranny. They took the Soviet road to freedom only to find it a snare and a delusion.

The fact that the reds have never contributed anything tangible to the progress of the Negro is overlooked though the reds have collected millions of dollars as a result of race incitement.

Like the Communist Party, the N.A.A.C.P. has collected millions of dollars through exploitation of race issues. The

RED PROMISES BROUGHT SLAVERY
U. S. NEGRO REDS REMAIN BLIND

New York Journal-American
Wed., June 6, 1956

'Utopia' Just an Illusion:

26 Negroes Who Went to Russia Homesick for U. S., Singer Reveals

By LORENZO FULLER
(As told to Martin Steadman)

Every night they clustered around the stage door of the Stanislavsk Music Theatre in Moscow.

They didn't have the price of admission to "Porgy and Bess," but every night they came just to talk to us after the show.

They are the 26 Negroes living in Moscow.

Fifteen years ago they had left their homes in America to come to this Russian "Utopia."

Now they want to come home—but cannot.

In 1941, these people sailed from America to settle in Russia. Possibly they were motivated by the feeling the grass was greener for them there.

Possibly they were impressed by the tremendous reception the Russians gave Paul Robeson on his tour a short time before.

We weren't invited to their homes. Maybe it wasn't permitted. But between questions, they told us a little about how they lived.

The men worked as laborers, delivery men and merchants. Their wives worked too.

Their clothes were no better than the average Russian's, which is to say they were pretty shabby.

They know by now the American system is the best system; that America is the land of opportunity and Russia is not.

They met us outside every night for two weeks. If we were still playing Moscow, I'm sure they'd be there tonight, asking the same questions they had asked before.

I keep thinking of these people. I keep thinking of the Biblical story of Jacob and Esau.

"They have sold their birthright for a mess of pottage."

The above excerpts are from an account given to the New York Journal-American by Lorenzo Fuller, a Negro member of the folk opera, "Porgy and Bess," when he played in Moscow in 1956. The tragic fate of Negro reds who went to the Soviet promised land seems to have made little impression on American reds—both Negro and white.

bigger the race issue, the bigger the appeal and the bigger the contributions. Last year, according to Roy Wilkins, the N.A.A.C.P. had the "greatest financial year in its history."

Yet one cannot find any report of any of this money being spent for factories and shops to provide jobs, land and home construction, specialized training for talented youth, hospitals, convalescent homes, classes in sanitation and personal hygiene, care and upkeep of property, combatting crime and juvenile delinquency, centers to aid Negro youth in preparing to meet stiff employment competition in science and industry.

It is then no accident that the N.A.A.C.P. is dubbed "The National Association for the Agitation of Colored People." The record speaks for itself. Millions for agitation; not one cent for those things that win the respect and acclaim of other races and national groups.

The N.A.A.C.P. set up the situation that erupted into racial violence at Little Rock, Arkansas. Reds all over the world dramatized the racial incidents created in Little Rock as examples of how white Americans resort to extremes of racial violence to deny Negroes an education. Every Communist Party in Asia and Africa, it seems, was alerted to "do a job" on America. At the same time here at home, they were screaming about the damage to our prestige abroad. Any way you look at it, it is a two-way pincer movement against Uncle Sam.

Therefore, we may readily assume that any damage done to our prestige abroad should be at the feet of the N.A.A.C.P. and the reds who started the trouble. What is significant is that those who spread the lie that violence erupted because Negro children are denied an education have not repudiated it.

Any confusion or misunderstanding created abroad has not been cleared up by the N.A.A.C.P. leadership. At no time have they admitted that no Negro in the United States is denied an education. And, too, they have not admitted that not every Negro wants an education, for reasons better known to himself. That accounts for many Negroes not being able to read or write. Moreover, there are free schools open both day and night for all those who want an education.

There are Negro institutions of higher learning and integrated ones, based upon geographical lines that make available the highest type of training for those Negroes who seek it. There are special scholarships and funds created by white philanthropists that enable Negroes to attend the finest universities and colleges in the country. What is ironic is that most of the Negro leaders responsible for the incitement of racial violence have been the recipients of these scholarships and grants. They possibly would have been cotton pickers or bootblacks were it not for this aid. Because only this aid gave them the free time to plot the destruction of America.

One can very well question the sincerity of the reds and the N.A.A.C.P. when they try to create the impression that America in general and the South in particular is a hell hole of despotism where the Negro is concerned. This is so since the whole issue boils down to taking Negro children out of one school and transferring them to another so that they can be seated with white children on the assumption that only in this way will the Negro child get an education.

What really is being implied is that the 113,000 Negro teachers in Southern schools are inferior, incompetent and unable to properly teach the children of their own race. Since it is no longer made a question of better schools, better facilities and equal pay, it is a question of liquidation of the Negro school and the Negro teacher under the guise of integration.

Naturally, white parents are going to resist any attempt to force them to send their children to school on an integrated basis when Negro teachers are considered unfit by members of their own race.

Maybe this is the reason why hundreds of Negro teachers were fired in the border and Southern states where there was token integration.*

It is also implied that a Negro child is handicapped in his studies unless he is sitting beside a white child. What could be more nonsensical or ridiculous? It is a sad commentary on the ability of the Negro child to say that he cannot properly study or that he will develop harmful complexes if he does not sit beside a white child. By what quirk of reasoning does one conclude that sitting beside a white child will help a Negro child make the grade? Experience shows that a student's success is determined by how much attention, time and effort he is willing to put into his studies.

In New York, for example, many Negro Junior High and High School graduates are outrageously poor in spelling,

---

* In the *Daily Worker*, official communist daily, Oct. 15, 1956, page 3, quotes the *N. Y. Times* as stating "That 500 Negro teachers lost their jobs in Southern and the border States due to integration." The *Pittsburgh Courier*, the largest Negro newspaper in America, April 19, 1958, carried the headline "Integration Leaves 300 Okla. Teachers Jobless."

500 NEGRO TEACHERS FIRED IN SOUTH, SURVEY FINDS

An estimated 450 to 500 Negro teachers have lost their jobs in Southern and border states, largely in rural areas where former all-Negro schools were closed, according to a New York Times survey revealed yesterday.

In Oklahoma, integration of 161 school districts out of 187 meant loss of jobs for 295 Negro teachers—and for no white teacher.

In Kentucky, 60 Negro teachers were dismissed; in West Virginia, 52. In South Carolina, a three-judge federal panel Oct. 22 will hear the case of 18 out of 24 Negro teachers

"Paradoxically, those states, that have made the greatest strides in ending segregation report the largest number of displaced Negro teachers," the Times said. While St. Louis, Louisville and other cities have employed displaced Negro teachers this apparently was done largely by putting them in remaining all-Negro schools.

In Washington Oct. 8 and 9, the plight of the ousted Negro teacher in the integration front was presented to spokesmen for the National Education Association by representatives of the American Teachers Association, Negro organization. NEA is to appoint a subcommittee to seek solutions.

ATA spokesmen said a majority of the Negro fired from teaching jobs are working elsewhere; while some went to Ohio, Indiana and other Northern states, some went into the Deep South where segregation continues.

The above, printed in the communist *Daily Worker*, is an excellent example of the flexible maneuvers carried on by the red apparatus on the racial battle-front. First, the reds have pushed through forcible integration through their leftist network. As a result hundreds of Negro teachers have lost their jobs. However, being skilled political manipulators, the reds jumped into the breach and now agitate among the very people who are the victims of the red inspired integration policy.

1955 admitted that Southern Negro children moving to New York City are on a level two grades higher than those in New York City schools.

What is also important to remember is that the late Dr. George W. Carver, the outstanding Negro scientist, was born of slave parentage. He did not learn to read and write until he was twenty. He worked his way through school to become one of the world's greatest scientists. He didn't have the opportunities of young Negroes today. Every difficulty was a challenge, so he had no time to develop complexes.

The main danger and handicap to the Negro is not the Southern school, but the persecution and hate complex the N.A.A.C.P. and the reds are trying to create.

Chapter Eight

MODERN DAY CARPET BAGGERS

At the root of all the present racial trouble is interference in the internal affairs of Southern States by people not at all interested in an amicable settlement of any problems arising between Negro and white Americans.

This interference comes from organizations and individuals in the North seeking to use the Negro. Among them are found Communists, crypto-communists, fuzzy-headed liberals, eggheads, pacifists, idealists, civil disobedience advocates, socialists, do-gooders, conniving politicians, self-seekers, muddle-headed humanitarians, addle-brained intellectuals, crackpots and plain meddlers. Like "missionaries," they descend on the South ostensibly to change or alter it to benefit the Negro.

In fact and in implication, all of them seek to by-pass the responsible white and Negro leaders in the South to effect a solution. They employ a pattern of setting up provocative situations which inflame and agitate the white populace and then using it as propaganda here and abroad against the South in particular and all of America in general.

White Southerners who oppose these "missionaries" are pounced upon and labeled "race baiters", "reactionaries", "Ku Kluxers", "white supremacists", "persons outside the law" and so forth.

Negro Southerners who oppose these "missionaries" are also attacked and labeled "Uncle Toms", "traitors of the race", "handkerchief heads", "white folks niggers" and so forth.

Obviously such name calling is a deliberate attempt on the part of these "missionaries" to scuttle all the progress made by the Negro since slavery by creating an atmosphere of distrust, fear, and hate. Like a witch stirring her brew the "missionaries" stir up all the sectional and racial bitterness that arose in the wake of the Civil War and Reconstruction. They open old wounds. They thumb the pages of closed chapters. They rake over the dying embers of old grudges, old grievances, old fears and old hates, that time has been gradually consigning to history in the onward sweep of a young, lusty, healthy and growing nation.

Labeling opponents is a specialty of the reds. *Smear is a cardinal technique.* Any label found in the red stockpile, you may be sure, is carefully made and selected to draw the maximum hate to the person or persons, the group or the organization to which it is attached.

The use of such labels has a tendency to divide America. Nothing, in my opinion, would please the aforementioned weird assortment of "missionaries" more than a divided America unless it is a Soviet America. They are forever predicting it at the same time working tirelessly to bring it about.

Moreover, while they talk about "racial strife" in America as providing grist for Moscow's propaganda mill they are busy creating it. They are careful to hide the fact that they are responsible for the provocations of extremists as was the case in Little Rock.

In all red propaganda, here and abroad, such acts of extremists are made the symbol of the treatment of the Negro in America. It also is the red smear pot in which all opponents of a "forthwith solution" of the race problem are tossed. The fact is that the majority of white Southerners are opposed to extremists. All-white Southern juries have convicted some of them as troublemakers and white Southern judges have sentenced some of them to long prison terms. This is deliberately ignored or played down by the leftists.

Mr. James P. Mitchell, Secretary of Labor, reported that the Department of Labor in a recent survey found that:

"Purchasing power of the Negroes was more than $17,-000,000,000 and that a third of the Negro population owned their own homes. Negro wage earners, he said, make four and a half times what they earned in 1940.

"He listed important gains by Negroes in ownership of banks, insurance companies, businesses, civil service employment and professional, skilled crafts and clerical and sales fields. In education, he said, Negro college enrollments have increased at a rate six times that of white students, while more than 98 per cent of Negroes between the ages of 7 and 13 are in school."*

These facts, too, are ignored or played down by the leftist "missionaries" and irresponsible crusaders. In political warfare, it seems, a cardinal principle to credit your enemy with only that which will hasten the build-up for his destruction.

The media of public information is far from free of communists and fellow travelers who operate under the guise

* *New York Times,* Wednesday, November 20, 1957.

of liberalism. They are ready at all times to do an effective smear job. Among these red tools may be found editorial writers, columnists, news commentators and analysts, in the press, radio and television. They go overboard in giving top news coverage to racial incidents, fomented by the leftists, and also those incidents that are interpreted so as to show "biased" attitudes of whites against Negroes. This is a propaganda hoax aimed, not at helping the Negro, but at casting America in a bad light in order to destroy its prestige and influence abroad, thereby aiding Soviet Russia in the penetration and conquest of Asia and Africa.

In the meantime the Negro is the sacrificial lamb—the innocent victim of the widespread racial hate which the leftists are creating. The energizing of race hate is an asset to the red cause. The more, the merrier, so long as it erupts in cross burnings, threats, loss of jobs, refusal of loans, boycotts, bombings, fist fights, beatings and shootings.

Thus all racial progress based upon understanding, goodwill, friendship and mutual cooperation, built up painfully over the years, is wiped out. White Americans are set against Negro Americans and vice versa. The stage is thus set for the opening of a dark and bloody era in Negro and white relations.

Many white Northern politicians objectively aid the rapidly deteriorating racial situation through the exploitation of leftist propaganda to garner Negro votes. They care not a tinker's dam about the Southern Negro and simply flatter the Northern Negro whom they consider a gullible fool. Getting elected and re-elected is their only concern.

Dishonorable mention should also be given to those white individuals and racial groups posing as friends of the Negro only to use him as a spearhead to attain certain objectives. They constitute in no small way the financial sinews of the movement. Naturally, they project programs and policies on those Negro tools who live off their largesse. Since "he who pays the piper calls the tune," could anything less than full submission be expected by these so-called Negro leaders? It does not matter to what extent Negro Americans generally feel the brunt of the racial hostility which these harmful programs engender, so long as the so-called Negro leaders win the approbation of their white masters and the money keeps rolling in.

Significantly, among all the aforementioned groups and individuals, there is only one highly organized, trained and disciplined force, and that is the Communists. So they are able to use, manipulate and combine this weird assortment of leftist "missionaries" in one way or another to bring about "a social upheaval which will plow up Southern institutions to their roots."

Indeed the spectre of the *"modern Carpet Bagger"* haunts the South. Reds, NAACPers, do-gooders and other "missionaries" follow in the footsteps of those Northerners who for narrow, selfish, personal or political reasons meddled in the affairs of the South in the period immediately following the Civil War. Like their predecessors, these *modern-day Carpet Baggers* create only mischief for they have no true interest in the South.

A check of the record of these *modern-day Carpet Baggers* will show that most of them are either Communists or persons who have been, or are now, associated with the Communist cause as a fronter, endorser, or fellow traveler.

Under the circumstances, it becomes the bounden duty of every government agency, in the interest of internal security, to reveal to the American people the record of each individual, regardless of race, creed, religion, position or rank, who is involved in inciting white and Negro Americans against each other.

Naturally, the opponents of the publication of such information are going to scream louder than ten thousand pigs caught under a fence. Charges of anti-Negro, anti-democratic bias will fill the air. "Old man Smear" will have a field day. In this way, as in the past, any real investigation of Communism or pro-Communism among Negroes is headed off, defeated or driven into a blind alley. Color and race thus becomes a sanctuary. On the one hand, patriotic and honest politicians and officials do not dare invade it critically without dire consequences to their personal reputations. On the other hand, this same "sanctuary" becomes the playground, not only of the reds, but of hypocrites, demagogues, bigots, self-seekers, opportunists, conniving politicians and other dregs of human society.

Too few Americans in our day have the courage of their convictions. Too few will fly in the face of leftist opposition. Too few will stand up for truth in the face of the ominous and destructive storm of "me-tooism" or the communist ideological regimentation that hangs like a pall over our country. Many take the attitude that it is better to be safe than sorry or conclude, after a little difficulty or several reverses, that "if you can't beat 'em, join 'em." The words *God, country* and *posterity* have lost much of their substance and are becoming only a shadow in the hearts and minds of many Americans.

Great Negro Americans such as Booker T. Washington and George Washington Carver should serve both as an inspiration and a reminder to the present and successive generations of Negro Americans that they too "can make their lives sublime and in departing leave behind them footprints in the sands of time."

The great surge of progress of the Negro since slavery can be largely traced to the work and efforts of these two men, their supporters, their emulators and their followers. Theirs was a deep and abiding pride of race, a firm belief in the ability of their benighted people to rise above their past and eventually stand on an equal plane with all other races. Moreover, equality was to them, not just a catch-word—the prattle of fools—but a living thing to be achieved only by *demonstrated ability*.

Chapter Nine

RACE PRIDE IS PASSÉ

The Negro business man has always been a chief target of the reds. They despise him because of his conservatism. They label him "a tool of the white imperialists" and an "enemy of the Negro masses." Such labels are reserved for those the reds plan to liquidate and since the Negro business man is an inspiration and example to other Negroes to take advantage of the countless opportunities of the free enterprise system, he is therefore an object of derision by Communists. An enthusiastic response of the Negro to the appeal and opportunities for Negro business is a cardinal bulwark against Communism. Consequently, the reds seek to discredit, discourage and liquidate Negro business.

Only during the period of the *Popular Front* did the reds cease their attack on Negro business in order to link the Negro banker, broker, realtor, business man, merchant, lawyer, physician, preacher, worker and farmer with Bolshevism under the guise of a *National Negro Congress*.

Basically, the reds' policy is now, and always has been, anti-Negro business. The fact that Negro business is sustained in the main by Negro patronage, that it exists almost entirely in the Negro community, makes it vulnerable to attack by the reds. They term it a product of "segregation," "social isolation," "the ghetto," etc. And, too, the reds use the example of sharp competition between small and big business to discourage Negro entry into the general arena.

While it is true that Negro businesses in only a few instances function outside the Negro community, this does not mean that they cannot function in other areas if the Negro provides attractive goods and services. But what is wrong with the Negro owning and operating community business? The Germans, the Italians, the Irish, the Jews, the Chinese have their respective communities where they own and operate most of the businesses. At no time do they consider it as a crime. Chinatown in New York and San Francisco are splendid examples of the community resourcefulness and pride that draw, like a magnet, multitudes from all walks of life. The Negro can learn much from the Chinese.

I recently attended a luncheon at the Hotel New Yorker in New York City, sponsored by a very fine and cultured group of Negro ladies. We were served in a private dining room by white waiters and waitresses. There was not a white person present except the hotel employees, yet these Negroes considered this integration. Any one of a number of Negro caterers could have supplied the same service. What is more important is that large sums paid to this hotel could have helped develop and expand a Negro catering service. Other races have such services which are not considered "integrated." Yet the Negro bitten by the integration bug is so naive that he thinks that boycotting his own race and spending his money in a place where he is unwanted and isolated is "putting his own best foot forward." One of the officers of the group said, "It's good to be seen in such places," as if some special honor had been conferred upon her. She was so carried away with the fact that she could walk through the lobby of a white hotel to a private (segregated) dining room that had I suggested that it did not mean acceptance, I would have made an enemy.

Other members waxed eloquent in their praise of those responsible for the decision to hold "our annual luncheon" in "white hotels" because it "leads toward integration." How I'll never understand. Nobody paid any attention to our coming. They had seen Negroes before. We were not too hard to be seen nor identified. We left the same way. There was no welcome mat; no enthusiastic reception. To me it seemed that the employees and management were glad to get rid of us.

The disastrous effect of "integration," so ardently advocated by the reds and the N.A.A.C.P. is evident in the following article:

"NEGRO BUSINESSMEN DISTURBED!

"Negro businessmen, such as hotel owners, tavern operators and sellers of cooked food, are up in the air in some cities because Negro money is bypassing their cash registers and falling into the pockets of white proprietors who run choice spots in downtown areas.

"This is especially true in the convention cities of Detroit and Miami. Detroit businessmen on the Negro side raised quite a howl a few months back when an all-Negro female conclave hit town and none of the delegates as much as looked through the doors of Negro-operated businesses. They slept in white-owned hotels, convened in white convention rooms, ate in white dining rooms, drank at white bars, and danced in white ballrooms.

"Owners and operators of Negro businesses in Miami, Fla., were quite angry last year after the African Methodist Episcopal Church General Conference packed up and got out of town. They claimed AME delegates, and there were hundreds of them, spent their money with white hotels on Miami Beach and even took their meals in Miami Beach restaurants. Negro taxicab drivers were pretty hot, too.

"Not too far back, Negro cab drivers chased a white cab driver out of Miami's Negro area because he was riding a Negro passenger.

"Somebody down in Miami must have talked to officials of the Church of God in Christ before they held their International Youth Conference there last week, because the conference was held in a Negro church, delegates lived in Negro hotels, ate in colored dining rooms, and held their banquets in big rooms made available by Negro hotels. They even held an open air festival at the all-Negro Virginia Beach just out of Miami."*

Betrayal of the Negro people may well come through Communist corruption of the Negro intellectual. This is not so difficult since the Communists, the "white liberals" and the "white progressives" do the thinking for most of them.

The utter bankruptcy of the Negro intelligentsia is startlingly evident by reason of the absence of any strong and dramatic movement for genuine Negro organization, leadership and thinking. Deep in the swamp of inferiority, lack of ability, muddled thought, the Negro intelligentisia looks to the phoney white liberals, politicians and progressive hypocrites for leadership, guidance and money. These "whites" are carriers of "isms" other than Americanism which spreads like an epidemic in the ranks of the hapless Negro intellectuals. Due to the lack of race pride, there is no immunity.

---

* *The Pittsburgh Courier* (the largest Negro newspaper in the U.S.), July 13, 1957, *Behind the Headlines*, by Robert M. Ratcliffe.

Chapter 10

WISDOM NEEDED

All other racial and national groups have their respective organizations. No Negro belongs to any of these organizations, nor is his membership sought or welcome. Moreover, no Negro is called upon to decide what is best for any one of these groups. What is most important is that no one of these groups considers itself "segregated" because no Negro belongs, is invited, nor has his opinion sought. Yet the Negro intellectual contends that to get together as Negroes, to discuss common problems as Negroes, to decide what is best for Negroes, without white participation, is "segregation."

Such an attitude speaks for itself. It is a hangover from slavery when the Negro had to depend on the master for everything necessary for his well being. At the same time, it proves that no "Proclamation of Emancipation" is capable of freeing those who do not wish to be free. The Negro intelligentsia, by far and large, is physically free but mentally slave. After nearly a century removed from chattel slavery, they are unwilling and incapable of throwing off their slave psychology. Reds and political charlatans of all shades, aware of this fact, find the Negro intellectual easy prey.

Fundamentally, there is deep racial consciousness among Negro Americans. They have, inspite of the divisive influence of the Negro intellectual, the same instinctive urge to group together as have other racial and national groups.

They desire progress through the medium of education, reliability, know-how and productivity, all so essential in competitive society. They know that to hold a comparable job they must be just as good and in most instances better, though a number of Negro intellectuals try to convince them that the cry of discrimination is a good substitute.

Furthermore, they know that a number of Negroes developed skills during the war, but that the great majority are not highly skilled or trained to fit into industry during this atomic age. (Thanks to W. E. B. DuBois and Monroe Trotter for their indefatigable toil to defeat the industrial training program of Booker T. Washington which would have made the Negro an indispensable part of American industry.)

Booker T. Washington's philosophy of education was to prepare the majority of Negroes through vocational training, to play a vital role in the rapidly developing American economy before and after the turn of the century. He undoubtedly foresaw the process of industrialization, the ensuing demand for trained, qualified personnel, i.e., skilled tradesmen who could be relied upon to do a job efficiently and well. Such training would enable the Negro to maintain his favored position, after slavery, and place him in a better competitive position against immigrants in the labor market. He stressed pride of race, home ownership, land ownership along with industrial and agricultural training.

Leftists, DuBois and Monroe Trotter bitterly assailed this philosophy. Consequently, most Negro youths avoided the skilled trades as "menial." According to Mr. Carter G. Woodson, the vacuum was filled by white immigrant labor.

Many Negroes realize that DuBois was wrong then, as he is today, in his attempt to steer them down the road to Communism. Further, the average Negro realizes that his happiness and well-being are not served to him on a silver platter, but come as a result of hard and difficult struggle. He therefore seeks (1) practical solutions to all his problems, and (2) a way to get along with other Americans with the least possible friction. Sagely, he realizes that a man cannot live constantly in the miasmic fog of race hostility without stifling to death, nor can he live fighting all other Americans all the time.

On the other hand, the vociferous Negro intellectuals, along with the reds, through their impractical, unrealistic, alien behavior, turn race relations into a shambles. Every Negro who opposes integration and the N.A.A.C.P. becomes a traitor or an "Uncle Tom." Every white person taking a similar stand is branded a "criminal" and "outside of the law." The fact that courts have been known to reverse themselves and that under our system of government every American has the right to protest and oppose any ruling considered onerous or prejudicial is ignored. Stupidly, they go about their business of forcing everybody to conform or be damned, thus building up fires of resentment that will require the work of centuries to extinguish.

Already, under the guise of "struggling for Negro rights," they have created all the explosive material for racial violence by making impossible demands, resisting sane and just decisions, opposing compromise and adjustment and demanding that everything must be done forthwith or not at all.

They have no love for their own people. They have no love for America. Naturally, they get the Kremlin's support and approval. Feeling frustrated and inferior, they run to communism and civil disobedience in their folly. They play Moscow's game and they deserve whatever red reward that is due them.

A WORLD VIEW OF RACE

by RALPH J. BUNCHE, PH.D.

Associate Professor of Political Science, Howard University

(1) If the oppressed racial groups, as a result of desperation and increasing understanding, should be attracted by the principles of equality and humanitarianism advocated by the Soviet Union (and it is both logical and likely that they will) then racial conflict will become intensified. In such case, however, racial conflict will be more directly identified with class conflict, and the oppressed racial groups may win the support of oppressed, though previously prejudiced, working-class groups within the dominant population

(2) It is only when this supremacy and privilege are dissolved and when it is no longer within the power of the privileged property-holding class to determine the institutional life and habits of the modern state, that there can be hope for the development of an international order and community which will promise the subject peoples of the world genuine relief from the heavy colonial burdens of imperialist domination.

(3) Race issues appear but tend to merge into class issues. Throughout the world the issue between working and owning classes is sharpening. The titanic conflicts of the future will be the product of the uncompromising struggles between those who have and those who have not. These conflicts now wage within all groups, racial and national. Insofar as the great masses of the black and yellow races are concerned, the status of economic and political inferiority which they have been compelled to accept results in their automatic identification with the working and "have not" classes of the society. They are now beginning to understand the true nature of the issues confronting them. Moreover, they will eventually appreciate the great possibilities in their numerical strength as a weapon in their struggle for justice. Their organized and directed support of the working class of the dominant populations of the world will bring an unchallengeable power to this class.

And so class will some day supplant race in world affairs. Race war then will be merely a side-show to the gigantic class war which will be waged in the big tent we call the world.*

---

1   The much louted Ralph Bunche (now a high official in the United Nations) spread the communist
    canard about the Soviet Union representing "principles of equality and humanitarianism."
2   Here Ralph Bunche, advocates the elimination of the "property owning class" from running the
    "modern" state." To him the "class struggle" = "to be the ultimate form of revolutionary warfare
3   This is the conclusion of Bunche's pamphlet. It is the same line that was expressed by Soviet leaders
    in their efforts to use the racial groups as cannon fodder in the struggle to master the earth."**

World View of Race, by Ralph J. Bunche, published in 1936 in Washington,
D. C., pages 36-61-63-98.

**See *The Leftist Background of Ralph Bunche*, published by The Alliance Inc.,
200 East 66th Street, New York 21, N. Y.

APPENDICES

Below are excerpts from the testimony of the Honorable James A. Cobb, a patriotic Negro American, former professor of Constitutional Law and vice dean of Howard University, in which he tried to alert America to the grave dangers to our internal security inherent in the advocacy of Communism by Mr. Mordecai W. Johnson, President of Howard University.

The failure to heed the sensational disclosures and timely warnings of Judge Cobb may well lie at the root of much of the present racial conflict.

TESTIMONY OF JAMES A. COBB

(The witness was duly sworn by the chairman.)

The CHAIRMAN. What is your name?

Mr. COBB. My name is James A. Cobb.

The CHAIRMAN. Are you an attorney?

Mr. COBB. I am.

The CHAIRMAN. State what institution or institutions and in what capacity you have been associated with them.

Mr. COBB. I have been connected with Howard University for a number of years; since 1916 as an instructor and professor of law at Howard University. I also acted as attorney for the university for a number of years. I was also on the university council for a number of years.

The CHAIRMAN. Have you held any appointive offices?

Mr. COBB. I have.

The CHAIRMAN. Will you please enumerate them?

Mr. COBB. I was designated by the late President Theodore Roosevelt as Special Assistant to the Attorney General, assigned to the United States Attorney's Office of the District of Columbia, and I served under Attorneys General Bonaparte, Wickersham, Mr. Justice McReynolds, and Attorney General Gregory.

The CHAIRMAN. Are you acquainted with Mordecai W. Johnson, now president of Howard University, Washington, D. C.?

Mr. COBB. I am.

The CHAIRMAN. Do you know what is the attitude of Mordecai W. Johnson, president of Howard University, toward communism?

Mr. COBB. I do, both from hearing him personally and from reading his published utterances.

The CHAIRMAN. Are you prepared to submit proof to the Committee on Un-American Activities of the fact that Mordecai W. Johnson, president of Howard University, has publicly advocated the doctrines of communism?

Mr. COBB. I am. I think that the evidence which I will offer to the committee, which consists of an investigation conducted by the Acting Secretary of the Interior, with respect to alleged communistic activities at Howard University in Washington, D. C., together with certain newspaper clippings reporting his addresses, and in addition the fact that I heard some of these statements made, in my opinion, will be sufficient to satisfy this committee that Mordecai W. Johnson, president of Howard University, has publicly advocated the doctrines of communism.

It has been shown by a governmental investigation that Mordecai W. Johnson and other officers of Howard University have misappropriated funds which were furnished to the university and that Howard University was required to pay back, from its endowment, over 40 thousand dollars to the Government of the United States.

From these facts I am convinced that when an institution is the recipient of over $600,000 annually of the taxpayers' money, and the head of that institution is endeavoring, through the advocacy of communism, to destroy the very Government whose largess he is receiving, that the president of that institution should be separated from his high office.

By virtue of the position of Dr. Johnson, as president of Howard University, he occupies an office of such preeminence that he is able to influence and mold the thoughts and political views of the future leaders of the colored race. Since Howard University is an institution, largely supported and maintained by the Federal Government, this is not a private affair, but is or should be a matter of national interest.

I love this country of ours. I think that I am a patriot. I have been honored by my people as its representative in public office. I am deeply grateful for the honors bestowed upon me as the representative of my people. It is solely with the thought of guarding and protecting their well being and the security of the United States that I appear before your committee to protest the communistic teachings of Dr. Mordecai W. Johnson, as president of Howard University.*

APPENDIX B

Professor Kelly Miller, another patriotic Negro American and former Dean of the College of Arts and Sciences, Howard University, was so alarmed at red activities at the University that, in order to alert America, he gave the following sworn affidavit:

EXHIBIT 1

CITY OF WASHINGTON,
  District of Columbia:
On this 27th day of June 1935 personally appeared before me, a notary public in the District of Columbia, Kelly Miller, of Washington, D. C., who, being first duly sworn, deposes and says:

That he is a graduate of Howard University and has been a professor and dean of the college at Howard University for 45 years, and at present is dean emeritus of said university.

That a conference on the economic condition of the Negro was held in Douglass Hall, Howard University, May 18, 19, 20, 1935. That he attended every session of this conference, and from the tenor of the opening he judged that the trend of the conference would be radical, leaning in the direction of communism, and he therefore queried the presiding officer as to whether it would be the purpose of the conference to keep the discussion within the framework of the Christian religion, democratic institutions, and the Constitution of the

*Testimony of Honorable Judge James A. Cobb before the House Committee on Un-American Activities at Washington, D.C., on November 5, 1938. Vol. No. 3, Pages 2142, 2143, 2144 and 2150.

United States. He was informed that there was no such intention.

Deponent further avers that President Mordecai W. Johnson, of Howard University, was present at the time he made this query and had nothing to say.

That at the session on Sunday afternoon, May 19, the conference was addressed by Mr. W. B. Dubois and Professor Dorsey and Harris, of the university faculty; and that James W. Ford, vice presidential candidate on the Communist ticket during the last Presidential election, asked permission to speak, and that he announced the well-known principle of communism to bring about revolution by force. Professors Harris and Dorsey urged that the Negro should join with the forces of labor to bring about his salvation.

Deponent further avers that thereupon he arose and stated that the only components of the labor forces that are willing and ready to unite with the Negro are those of radical or communistic leanings, and that it would be suicidal for the Negro to ally himself with any force intent upon upsetting the Constitution and promoting revolution. In reply to these remarks two speakers passionately urged revolution through bloodshed, and one of them stated in vehement tones that without shedding blood, there could be no remission of sin. Mr. Waldron, Washington correspondent of the *Daily Worker,* a communistic organ, stated not only once, but twice: "The revolution is coming notwithstanding the F. D. Roosevelts and the Kelly Millers."

President Johnson presided at this session and heard the discussion, but made no comments of any kind or character.

At the closing session on Monday afternoon, which was

devoted to remedies for the Negro's economic condition, the listed speakers were Norman Thomas, candidate for the Presidency on the Socialistic ticket; James W. Ford, and a Mr. McKinney, representative of the American Labor Party, which is perhaps the most radical of them all. His name was inserted in the original program. Each of these speakers gave the remedies proposed by his party, all of which suggestions were revolution, with and without the use of force. There was no speaker listed to represent the New Deal or the existing democratic order.

Deponent avers that he arose and stated that this seemed to be an unfair and one-sided arrangement; since only radicals were asked to give remedies and left no place for the conservatives and New Dealers. He was informed by the presiding officer that several such representatives had appeared on the program during the session and he deemed this sufficient to represent their point of view.

Deponent left the sessions with the feeling that the whole purpose and trend of the conference was to discredit existing institutions in favor of radicalism or some form of revolution.

KELLY MILLER.

Subscribed and sworn to before me this 27th day of June 1935.

SAMUEL E. LACY,
Notary Public.
My commission expires on the 10th day of July 1938.*

---

*Report of the Hearings, House Un-American Activities Committee, Vol. No. 3, page 2148, Oct.-Nov., 1938.

*The U. S. Department of Labor made an investigation of red
activities at Howard University. Mr. Lawrence A. Oxley, Labor
Department investigator submitted the following "Memorandum"
on the national conference, which he attended at Howard University, in connection with the formation of the red National
Negro Congress. Note the fact that Ralph Bunche was listed as
one of the key left wingers leading that conference. Bunche
was an associate professor of political science at the time.*

On June 26, 1935, a memorandum was prepared by
Lawrence A. Oxley, of the United States Department of
Labor, Bureau of Labor Statistics, which is found on page
54 of Senate Document No. 217, Seventy-fourth Congress,
second session, which reads as follows:

UNITED STATES DEPARTMENT OF LABOR,
BUREAU OF LABOR STATISTICS,
Washington, July 26, 1935.

Memorandum to Mr. Humphrey:

(Mr. Humphrey was the Government agent who was
making an investigation at that time of the communistic
activities at Howard University.)

It is my confirmed opinion that the national conference
held at Howard University May 18, 19, and 20, under the
auspices of the joint committee on national recovery and
the social-science division of Howard University—having
as its theme The Position of the Negro in our National
Economic Crisis—was distinctly communistic in character.

The opinion offered in this statement is based on my personal attendance and observations of every session of the

conference, beginning May 18 at 9:30 a.m., and closing May 20 at about 6 p.m.

With perhaps three or four exceptions, each speaker and discussant on the program seemed to be concerned first with making an attack on not only the present administration but American ideals and institutions. I believe that the last session of the conference is indicative of the trend and purpose of calling this meeting. Following the 3 days of speaking, discussions, and conferences, there seemed to be but "three ways out for the Negro. 1. The answer of the Socialist Party; 2. The answer of the Communist Party; 3. The answer of the American Labor Party"; Mr. McKinney.

With the exception of Mr. T. Burham King, the critical summaries of the conference were made by Mr. Reginald Johnson, Dr. Ralph Bunche, Mr. John P. Davis, and Mr. Emmett Dorsey. I believe that answers to the question, "What was the purpose of the conference?" are very well stated by a close study of the activities, utterances, and writings of the persons who made the critical summaries of the conference.

During the course of the last session, May 20, I heard Mr. Ford and Mr. Dorsey advocate the overthrow of the American Government, if necessary, to secure the objectives of the program sponsored by the conference.

(Signed) LAWRENCE A. OXLEY.*

APPENDIX D

The national conference held at Howard University, May 18, 19, 20, 1935, referred to in the testimony of Judge James A. Cobb was

---

* (Reference—page 2149, hearing held before the House Committee on Un-American Activities, Volume 3, October, November, 1938.)

held under the auspices of the "Joint Committee on National Recovery" and the "Social Science Department of Howard University." Ostensibly called to consider the "plight of the Negro under the New Deal" the conference actually served as a cover for the Kremlin's biggest and boldest operation among Negroes in America.

Consistent with the "new" Moscow line known as the "popular front," first tried and successfully developed in France, the Communist International ordered all of its sections to apply it in their respective countries. This new line based as it was on the strategy of the Trojan Horse was aimed at broadening and extending the base and influence of communism through infiltration and eventual capture of non-communist organizations.

This writer sat in on meetings of the National Committee, the Politburo and also the Negro Commission of the Communist Party in 1934 and 35 when the new line was discussed in relation to the Negro. The chief topic was how to bring the NAACP, Urban League, Elks, women's groups, youth, religious and labor organizations into a deceptive "democratic front" to advance the cause of communism among large, influential and decisive segments of the Negro people. Out of these discussions came the recommendations on how best to carry out Moscow's order to build a National Negro Congress in America.

Howard University was selected as one of the initiators and the site of the conference for two reasons,

1. *The reds had successfully won over not only the president but influential members of the faculty.*

2. *The prestige of the University situated as it is in Washington would give the launching of the project respectability and import.*

The executive head of the Joint Committee on National Recovery was John P. Davis, a red, who was later elected to the National Committee of the Communist Party. He was little known, at the time, except in top circles as a member of the Communist Party. It was for this reason he was brought into the picture along with the organization he headed. When the Negro Congress was formed in 1936 in Chicago, John P. Davis was elected National Secretary.

[74]

The following quotations taken from official communist and leftist sources substantiate much of this writer's own experience and knowledge.

Two months before the May, 1935 meeting in Howard University was held to mobilize communist infiltration into masses of Negroes, the Central Committee of the Communist Party of the U.S.A. declared to all of its members in a special communique:

"In connection with the question of the united front on the Negro question—if we work properly now and see that we must penetrate these organizations, there is the possibility of building up a National Negro Congress on a broad united front basis. We had a discussion about this conference in the N. Y. District in which we discussed the Negro question, and the possibility of a National Negro Congress. If we make the proper orientation, we will be able to build the biggest Congress of Negro people ever held. It means patient work in Negro organizations."[*]

The May, 1935 conference in Howard University was acknowledged by the communist high-command as a starting point for the National Negro Congress. Ralph Bunche, now a high official in the U.N., was given credit for being one of the chief organizers of this communist instrument to subvert American Negroes. In fact, in 1940 Bunche wrote a study for the Carnegie Foundation boasting of the part he played in initiating the National Negro Congress and stated that the Congress grew out of meetings in his own home and conferences in Howard University in 1935.[**] Official communist sources had the following to say about the birth of the National Negro Congress:

"It may be remembered that the National Negro Congress was proposed last May at a national conference held in Washington.

"There were other speakers who made valuable contributions on the plight of the Negro at the May Conference at Washington. Space will not permit us to quote from all of them. Among these were: Dr. Ralph J. Bunche, of Howard University; Lester Granger, of the Workers Council of the National Urban League; A. W. McPherson, of the Steel and Metal Workers Union; John McKinney, of the Southern Tenant Farmers' Union; Olive M. Stone, of the North Carolina Institute of Social Science."***

The development of the National Negro Congress as the instrument of swinging thousands of Negroes behind Soviet Russia was openly admitted to be a purely communist operation by the communists themselves as demonstrated by the following declaration:

"It is equally beyond dispute that the pioneering and trail-blazing work of the Communists has played a great part in opening the road towards the now developing broad people's movement. Our Party as a whole can justly take pride—not to rest in self satisfaction—in the role it played and is playing in awakening the Negro people, in helping to organize them, in bringing forth such Negro leaders as Ford and Herndon, and in promoting that united and people's front for Negro rights which resulted in the creation of the National Negro Congress."****

---

*Party Organizer, March, 1935, Vol. VIII, No. 3, issued by the Central Committee of the Communist Party, to all its membership. Article: "How to Penetrate the Negro Organizations." Excerpts from Report to Plenum. Page 21.

**Reference—the "Myrdal-Carnegie studies on the Negro question," by Ralph Bunche, 1940.

***The Communist, April 1936, Vol. XV, No. 4, page 322. Article: "The National Negro Congress" by James W. Ford, Negro member of the Communist Party Central Committee.

****The Communist, March, 1936, Vol. XV, No. 3, page 202. "Review of the Month."

Today, twenty years after Judge Cobb's sensational exposure of red activities at Howard University, this same university played host to one of the most rabid pro-Soviet propagandists in the country. Failure of the government to clean out, the red tools combined with the recent U.S. Supreme Court's rulings has made the sub-versives in Howard University more audacious than ever.

The excerpts below from the Negro newspaper, *The Afro-American*, in both the news article and editorial shows the contempt with which our Nation is held by those who lecture to the students and faculty.

THE AFRO-AMERICAN, APRIL 12, 1958

LECTURE AT HOWARD
'America fighting world progress,' DuBois declares

WASHINGTON

"The nation is headed wrong. It is not the first time a nation has been wrong, but it may be the last. . . ."

Thus declared Dr. William E. B. Du-Bois, noted scholar, author and pioneer in the battle for equal rights for minorities, as he concluded a 30-minute lecture at Howard University's Andrew Rankin Memorial Chapel, Monday night.

Speaking before a standing room crowd of more than 600 students, faculty members and visitors, Dr. DuBois outlined "A History of the last 40 years" as he saw it, and then stressed where "we stand in 1958."

On the latter point, the 90-year-old scholar declared "Today the United States is fighting world progress; progress which must be toward socialism and against colonialism and war."

He continued: "Socialism is inevitable, and communism is one way to achieve it. But, whether it is achieved by communism dictatorship or by democracy, its aim of giving to each what he needs and demanding what best he can give, is the inevitable aim of civilization and sooner or later will triumph."

Answering his own question, "Where now do colored people stand?" Dr. Du-Bois declared: "If we aim to be Americans, willing to do only what America does, think as it thinks and say what it says we are stupid."

DR. DuBOIS' lecture was sponsored by the Division of Social Sciences at Howard. Dr. Eugene C. Holmes, associate professor of philosophy and chairman of the Division of Social Sciences, said the visit to Howard was a tribute to him on his 90th birthday. (He celebrated his 90th birthday last month.)

Dr. DuBois at Howard

An Editorial

The Department of Social Sciences of Howard University deserves a great deal of credit for its courage in bringing the distinguished sociologist, author and scholar, Dr. W. E. B. DuBois to deliver an address to the students last week.

Critics of Dr. DuBois accuse him of being pro-communist and his speech Monday night did little to allay their suspicions, but there is one important factor which his critics overlook. Dr. DuBois is not saying anything now which he was not saying 40 years ago, long before the Russian revolution became a fait accompli

There are a number of compelling reasons why Howard University had no choice but to invite Dr. DuBois to their forum. As one of the pioneers in founding the Niagara Movement and the NAACP, he helped to crystalize the spirit which has brought the race a long way in its struggle for citizenship. As a founder of the Pan-African Conference, his writings fired the imagination of the young native leaders whose courage has brought about the evolution of several independent nations, with more to follow.

As a scholar and thinker, he is one of the darker men whom the white man fears. Howard University students were entitled to see and hear a man while he is still among us.

CPSIA information can be obtained
at www.ICGtesting.com
Printed in the USA
LVHW082111100620
657786LV00027B/2830